# The Secret of the Silver Shoes

Written by Elizabeth Massie
Illustrated by Bridget Starr Taylor

## STECK-VAUGHN
ELEMENTARY · SECONDARY · ADULT · LIBRARY

A Harcourt Classroom Education Company

www.steck-vaughn.com

# Contents

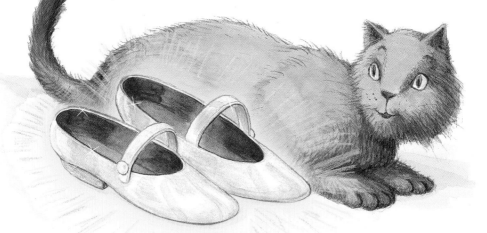

# Chapter 1

# Disappearing Act

"I'm tired of people thinking I'm you!" Piper West said in an angry voice. She paced back and forth across the kitchen floor.

Taylor, her twin sister, munched on a pickle and petted their cat, Clyde. "Piper, we're identical twins," she replied. "We look exactly alike. We can't change that."

"We *try* to look different," said Piper. "I like to wear pink. You like to wear blue. I have hair clips, but you have a hair band. I wear a necklace. You don't. But people still get us mixed up!"

3

Taylor shrugged. "You should be used to it after all these years."

"One more year on Saturday," Piper added with a sigh. "Another year of identical birthday presents. Nobody ever remembers that I love playing basketball, and you love playing soccer."

"How was school, kids?" asked Mom as she walked into the kitchen.

"Fine," answered Taylor.

"*Not* fine," said Piper. "Mrs. Gumbly said she liked my report on whales, but Taylor wrote that report. My report was about chimpanzees! We've been in her class for three months. She should know me by now!"

"Be patient," said Mom. "Everyone makes mistakes, even adults."

"It's hard being a twin," complained Piper. "I want people to remember who *I* am. I wish people would treat me special!"

Mom ruffled Piper's hair. "You're special to us and your friends."

"But I don't feel special," said Piper. "Maybe I should get my hair cut really short. Maybe I should get my ears pierced—" Piper's voice trailed off as her mother held up her hand like a traffic cop.

"Being special," Mom stated, "comes from inside you."

"Quit complaining," Taylor told Piper. "Have a pickle."

Piper took a pickle from the jar and bit into it unhappily. She didn't feel special inside or out.

"I'm going to the grocery store," Mom said. "Dad's in the family room. Do your homework before you do anything else."

"Okay," the girls said together, but Piper's voice was still grumpy.

They both had math homework. Taylor finished first, as always. "Come play soccer with me," she suggested.

"I don't feel like it right now." Piper scratched Clyde's ears. "And I need to finish my homework."

"Okay," answered Taylor. "See you later." The screen door banged shut as she ran outside.

Piper finished her homework, then headed up to the attic. It was her favorite place to go when things bothered her. Clyde followed her, padding silently up the stairs.

Opening the door to the attic, Piper paused while her eyes adjusted to the darkness. The huge, dusty place overflowed with boxes, clothes, and the thick smell of mystery. She plopped down on an old wooden trunk, and Clyde jumped in her lap.

"Nobody would miss me if I just disappeared," Piper said. "They'd just think Taylor was me."

Clyde yawned and licked a paw.

"I wish I were different, Clyde," she said to the cat. "I want to be special in my own way."

Piper sat on the trunk, deep in thought. She was stroking the fur on Clyde's back when she heard him growl low in his throat. He jumped off Piper's lap and trotted off.

*I bet he heard a mouse*, Piper thought to herself as she followed Clyde. He slipped through towers of boxes. Then he headed for a jungle of musty coats against a wall of the attic. As Piper got closer to the coats, she heard a soft, tinkling music. The beautiful notes tugged at her heart.

"Clyde?" Piper called. She was almost at the source of the music now. Clyde let out a meow, and she saw that he was staring at a shoebox.

The odd music was coming from it. Clyde sniffed the shoebox, and immediately it began to glow with a strange light. The music grew louder. Then the top slid back.

Piper blinked and rubbed her eyes. Inside the shoebox lay a pair of sparkling silver shoes.

"Wow," Piper whispered. She reached inside and picked up a shoe. The music stopped. She turned the shoe this way and that. *Whose shoes are these?* she wondered. *They look new, so why are they up here in the attic?*

9

Piper took off her sneakers and slipped one of the silver shoes on. It fit perfectly. She put on the other shoe. It was just right, too. *They feel like they were made just for me!* she said excitedly to herself.

Piper hurried to an old mirror and stepped in front of it. Clyde rubbed against her legs, a purr rumbling in his chest. She couldn't see anything, so she used an old bathrobe to wipe off the dust. Now she could see Clyde and everything else in the attic, but not herself. Piper waved her arms. Nothing.

"This is weird," she said aloud. Clyde looked at her and blinked mysteriously. Piper bent close to the mirror. Her breath fogged the glass. She stomped her foot, and Clyde ran for cover. There was still no reflection of her in the mirror.

Slowly the truth dawned on Piper. The shoes had made her disappear!

# Chapter 2

## Tricking Taylor

"I'm invisible!" Piper cried. Clyde jumped onto the back of a broken chair, his fur puffed out and ears flat.

Piper twirled around the attic in her magic silver shoes. As she danced close to the front window, she heard Taylor outside. Piper looked out and saw her sister kicking the soccer ball around on the driveway. She thought for a minute. Then a sly little smile played across her lips. *This will be fun!* she said to herself and headed for the attic door.

Piper tiptoed downstairs. In the family room, she waved her arms wildly and stuck out her tongue at her father. He didn't react. Piper grinned and headed for the front yard. Outside, three of their friends had joined Taylor to play soccer. No one saw Piper standing beside the driveway, not even her twin sister.

"Let's play!" yelled Eva.

Taylor and Mark teamed against Eva and Sam. They kicked the ball back and forth across the yard. Then Mark got control of the ball and kicked it past Sam.

Mark and Taylor cheered. Eva and Sam just shook their heads. Then Piper got in the act.

As Taylor aimed the ball, Piper stepped in and kicked it hard. The ball flew across the front yard.

"What happened?" asked Mark.

"Guess my foot slipped," said Taylor.

"Our ball!" Sam yelled.

The game started again. This time, when Taylor prepared to kick the ball past Sam, Piper kicked it in the opposite direction. It shot past a very surprised Mark.

"What?" Taylor gasped.

"The ball went the wrong way!" yelled Eva. "How'd that happen?"

"Maybe the wind blew it," replied Mark.

"Our point!" yelled Sam. "I'm glad you're not on my team, Taylor!"

Taylor frowned and wiped her forehead. "I'll try harder," she promised Mark.

The game went on. Sometimes Piper let Taylor make a goal, and sometimes she blocked the ball so that it bounced away.

"What is going on, Taylor? You used to be the best soccer player of us all," said Eva.

"Not anymore," said Sam.

"You're just having a bad day, Taylor." Mark patted her shoulder.

"I don't know what's wrong," Taylor said, frowning. "It doesn't make any sense."

"Tomorrow will be better," Mark said.

"Tomorrow I'll wear my soccer shoes," Taylor told Mark. "Maybe that'll help."

*Not if I'm wearing my silver shoes tomorrow,* Piper thought. She giggled, covering her mouth. *This is so much fun! They have no idea I'm here!*

The game ended with Eva and Sam winning. After everyone left, Taylor walked in the house and plopped down on a chair in the family room.

Piper followed her sister inside and stood next to her. *Taylor shouldn't take it so seriously,* she told herself. *It's just a joke. A little trick never hurt anyone.*

"Have fun playing?" asked Dad.

"No," answered Taylor. "I played terribly."

"You'll do better next time," said Dad. "You're a good soccer player."

Piper walked to the room she shared with Taylor. The shoes felt a little tight as she sat down on the floor to take them off. She hid them in her backpack and came back into the family room. "Hi!" she said to Taylor. "What's new?"

"Nothing," Taylor said glumly, "except that I'm terrible at soccer now."

"Gee, I'm sorry to hear that," Piper said insincerely. "You know, the right shoes can make a difference." *Especially if they're silver shoes,* she added silently.

Taylor looked hurt but didn't reply.

# Chapter 3

# Surprising Mrs. Gumbly

The next morning Piper couldn't wait to go to school. She had plans for more tricks. She'd told her mom and Taylor that she was going early to help their teacher feed Harley, the class hamster.

Down the sidewalk Piper ran alone, the shoes clicking together in her backpack. When she reached the classroom, she peeked inside. Mrs. Gumbly sat at her desk, marking math papers and eating a jelly doughnut. No one else was in the room yet.

Piper began to put on the silver shoes. They still felt a little tight, like they did when she took them off the night before. But she hurriedly pushed her feet in them. *It's okay if they're a little uncomfortable. It's worth it if I can be invisible,* she told herself.

Mrs. Gumbly didn't look up from her work. She had no idea she wasn't alone. Her marking pen made little scritch-scritch sounds on the papers.

Piper moved around the room as quietly as Clyde stalking a mouse, picking up the chairs and putting them on the desks. Meanwhile Mrs. Gumbly kept on grading papers, not noticing a thing. Mrs. Gumbly was famous for her powers of concentration.

When all the chairs were on the desks, Piper stomped on the floor. Mrs. Gumbly glanced up. "What in the world?" she exclaimed when she saw where the chairs now were.

Piper grinned broadly.

While Mrs. Gumbly put the chairs back on the floor, Piper hid Mrs. Gumbly's jelly doughnut on top of the filing cabinet. Back at her desk, Mrs. Gumbly looked around, then scratched her head. "Now where did I put that doughnut?" she wondered aloud.

Piper doubled over, trying not to laugh out loud. Mrs. Gumbly dug around in her desk, searching for the missing doughnut. Piper looked around for another trick to play. Then she spied the line leader list on the chalkboard. At the top of the list was the name of the class bully, Joe Blevins. It was his turn to be line leader.

*Joe doesn't deserve to be line leader today,* Piper decided. *I think it'll be my turn.* She switched her name and Joe's name, writing each one slowly to make her handwriting look like Mrs. Gumbly's.

Mrs. Gumbly found the doughnut on the filing cabinet. "When did I put it there?" she asked aloud.

Suddenly the morning bell rang, and Piper could hear students crowding into the hallways.

She grabbed her backpack and dashed into the restroom. "Ooh!" she said when she pulled off the silver shoes. "It feels good to get these things off." She looked in the mirror and saw that she was visible once more. She tucked the shoes into her backpack and put on her sneakers.

LINE LEADER
PIPER
MARY
BILL
FELIX

NICKY
OSCAR

In the classroom Joe said angrily, "It's my turn to be line leader. You wrote my name at the top of the list yesterday afternoon, but now Piper's is there. It's not fair to change the names, Mrs. Gumbly!"

Mrs. Gumbly studied the list closely, then bit her lip. "That's strange, Joe. I thought I wrote your name at the top, too, but we must be wrong. Some strange things have been happening around here," she said with a frown.

Piper had to bite the inside of her cheek to keep from laughing. She'd tricked two people with one joke! *That* was pretty special!

"So I'm line leader," Joe said smugly.

"No," Mrs. Gumbly said, "I'm sorry. That looks like my handwriting. I must have written Piper's name instead of yours."

Joe pointed at Piper. "Maybe she changed it. It's my turn!"

"Settle down, young man," Mrs. Gumbly said firmly. "Piper's name is first on the list, so it will be her turn today. You will be line leader on Monday."

*On Monday I'll wear my silver shoes again and make someone else line leader,* Piper decided. *It has to be okay to trick a bully more than once.*

"It's not fair," whined Joe. He slumped down into his chair.

*Yea!* Piper cheered silently. *I get to be first to music, first to play outside, and best of all, first to lunch!*

# Chapter 4

# Flying Flowerpots

After school Piper came home and went into the family room. She sat down in her favorite chair and petted Clyde, thinking up new tricks.

Mom walked in with Taylor. "Come on, Piper. We're going to the party store to pick out a few decorations for tomorrow."

"You mean we're going to have a big birthday party after all?" Piper asked excitedly.

Taylor shook her head. "I've tried and tried to talk Mom into letting us have one, but—"

"I've already told you both," Mom broke in. "I don't have time for a huge party this year. Just family tomorrow. Maybe next year you can have a big party."

"Come on, Piper, go with me," Taylor urged. "We don't want Mom to pick out anything nerdy."

"You go ahead," Piper replied. "I need to do my homework."

"All right," said Mom. "Dad's in the garage, so listen for the doorbell. Mrs. Carmelo said she was bringing over some birthday presents for you and Taylor. Be sure to thank her. It would be nice if you'd invite them over for birthday cake and ice cream tomorrow night."

Mr. and Mrs. Carmelo lived next door and raised all kinds of plants in their greenhouse. Piper had often helped the Carmelos water their flowers and vegetables.

Piper watched out the window as her mother and Taylor left. "Hey Clyde," she whispered, "let's get the silver shoes and see what the Carmelos are up to. This could be fun."

Quickly Piper got the silver shoes from her backpack and took off her sneakers. She struggled to slip on the shoes. They were tighter now. Piper tugged until they finally slipped on. Her feet ached when she stood, but a quick trip to the mirror in her bedroom told her they were still working. She was invisible again.

*Are these shoes shrinking?* Piper wondered as she headed for the Carmelos' backyard. *I haven't gotten them wet. I haven't even let them out of my sight!*

From inside the greenhouse, Piper could hear Mr. Carmelo whistling. She was going to have some more fun! It really didn't matter that the shoes were hurting her feet. She was only going to wear them long enough to play a trick or two.

Inside the steamy greenhouse, Mr. Carmelo watered a row of ferns hanging from the ceiling. He tapped his toes as he whistled.

Piper tiptoed to a shelf that stored empty clay flowerpots. Picking up two, she ran around Mr. Carmelo.

Mr. Carmelo couldn't believe his eyes. He dropped the water hose and stared at the pair of flowerpots hanging in the air. His mouth fell open as he watched them circle around him. The water hose flopped around, spraying water over the floor and the walls.

"What is this?" he cried in shock. "What is happening here?"

Piper picked up two more flowerpots and tried to juggle all four. She knew how to juggle three things, but not four. One pot crashed to the floor and broke in pieces. Mr. Carmelo touched the pot carefully. "This cannot be real," he said in a whisper. "This has to be my imagination."

Then Piper sat on the greenhouse floor and spun the three pots like tops. Swoosh, swoosh! That was enough for Mr. Carmelo. "Margaret!" he called out the door of the greenhouse. "Come quick! Come and look at this!"

Mrs. Carmelo stuck her head in the doorway. "Look at what?" she asked.

When Mr. Carmelo pointed to where Piper sat, Piper stopped spinning the pots.

"So you broke a pot," his wife said. "Why did you call me out here to see that?"

"I didn't break it," Mr. Carmelo replied. "It flew through the air and spun in circles. Then it broke itself."

"Flying flowerpots?" Mrs. Carmelo asked. She walked over to her husband.

"Spinning ones, too," he added.

Mrs. Carmelo smiled. "Edgar, you've always had a wild imagination."

"They were flying and spinning, I tell you," Mr. Carmelo insisted.

"We'll call the doctor for an appointment to get your eyes checked," Mrs. Carmelo said. She got a broom and a dustpan and began to clean up the broken flowerpot.

"My eyes don't need to be checked," Mr. Carmelo said sadly. "It was not my imagination." With a worried look on his face, he turned off the water hose.

Piper sneaked out of the greenhouse without a sound.

# Shrinking Shoes

On Saturday morning Piper and Taylor got up early. Dad was taking them ice skating for their birthday. He wished them a happy birthday and reminded them that they would have a little family party that evening. Piper put the silver shoes in her skate bag—just in case she saw a chance for another trick.

Skate City would have been more fun if their friends had been there. Piper and Taylor usually went on Sunday afternoons, but they knew that their friends usually skated on Saturday mornings.

"I don't see anyone we know," Piper commented as they skated. "Where's Sam? And Mark and Eva?"

"I don't know," Taylor answered, glancing around the rink. "I wonder where they are."

After skating, Dad took Piper and Taylor out for ice cream. Then they headed home.

"How was skating?" Mom stood at the door as the girls climbed out of the car.

"Okay," said Taylor. "But none of our friends were there. Not one!"

"Maybe they had something else planned this morning," replied Mom.

"All of them?" Taylor asked doubtfully as she and Dad walked inside.

Mom shrugged, then turned to Piper. "Aren't you coming in?" she asked.

"Yes," Piper said, "but I have to do something first." She clutched the bag with the shoes. *It's time for some real fun,* she said to herself. *I think Taylor needs a birthday trick.*

"Is it important?" Mom asked. "I have some things I need you to do. The kitchen needs to be swept, and the backyard needs to be mowed."

"It is, Mom. I'll be quick," Piper promised her mother.

Mom closed the front door, and Piper dashed to the garage with her skate bag. All she had to do was get the silver shoes on. She sat down in a dark corner and took them out of the bag. Hurriedly she began to shove the left shoe on.

"Ouch!" The shoe felt like it was biting her. Piper gritted her teeth. She pulled. She tugged. The shoe was painfully tight. "I WILL get these shoes on!" Piper vowed.

She stood up and stomped hard until she had crammed the left shoe on. She heard her parents call her name, but she didn't answer. She was too

busy trying to get the right shoe on, and it was even tighter than the left one. At last she forced her foot into it. Her feet throbbed. Limping slowly, Piper opened the door to the house.

There in the family room was the biggest surprise birthday party Piper had ever seen. Presents and a huge cake filled a table. A pink banner read "Happy Birthday, Piper and Taylor!" Their friends were shouting "Happy Birthday!" and "Surprise!" Balloons and streamers hung from the ceiling.

"Where's Piper?" Mark asked Taylor.

*Right here,* Piper thought, *except you can't see me.* Suddenly, being invisible wasn't that much fun. Playing another trick on Taylor didn't feel all that great, either.

"She's always late," said Sam.

Mom walked out to the garage. "Piper? Where are you?" she called.

Piper didn't answer, of course. She stood next to Mom, but nobody knew it.

"Piper?" her mother called again, beginning to sound worried. "Why isn't she answering me? Where could she be?"

"She'll turn up sooner or later," said Dad.

"What about the party?" Mom asked.

"Let's start without her," Dad suggested. "I'll cut the cake."

"I'll save her a piece," Taylor said. "I wish she'd hurry up and get here!"

Piper could almost taste the birthday cake. *Time to change shoes and reappear. I'll miss my own party if I don't hurry!* she told herself.

# Chapter 6

# Reappearing Act

Piper squeezed out the door just before her mother closed it. Then she hobbled into the garage to take off the shoes. But the shoes wouldn't come off. She tugged, she pulled, and she yanked. The shoes didn't budge. They were stuck to her feet like silver glue.

Piper limped out of the garage, trying not to cry. She had to figure out some way to get out of these awful shoes! She sat down beside the driveway and tried to think calmly. That was when she saw Lacy and Sabrina, two kindergarteners that lived up the street. Lacy was crying, and Sabrina was trying to comfort her. Piper hobbled painfully over to hear what was going on.

"Joe took my puppy!" Lacy sobbed. "He won't bring her back!"

35

"Joe Blevins is just trying to play a mean trick," Sabrina said. "He won't keep Princess. He just wants to make you cry."

*Joe's mean trick worked,* Piper thought. Lacy cried even harder.

Piper knew Joe lived on the next block. With every step stabbing her feet, she walked to Joe's house and stopped at the gate. In the backyard Princess was tied to a tree. She yapped and whined, trying to get away. Joe spun circles in a tire swing. "Hush up," he yelled at the upset puppy.

Piper opened the gate and walked over to the frightened puppy. Quickly she untied the leash and scooped Princess up. She knew Princess looked as if she were flying.

Joe stopped spinning. His eyes bulged out, and his mouth hung open like a bigmouth bass. Piper would have laughed in Joe's face if her feet hadn't hurt so much. She walked the puppy back to Lacy.

"Princess!" Lacy grabbed her puppy and hugged it. Sabrina smiled and patted Lacy's shoulder.

At Lacy's shout of joy, Piper noticed that the silver shoes felt a little less painful, though they still stuck to her feet.

"If you can't make a shot, then go home! Baby!" rang out loud voices across the street. Piper turned to see what was happening. Three boys were teasing Leo, the shortest kid in her class. The boys had blocked all Leo's basketball shots.

*I can help him!* Piper said to herself. *I'm the best basketball player on my team!* She hurried across the street in the tight shoes.

Just then, Joe Blevins ran up, panting. "You won't believe it, guys!" he said. "I saw a dog float through the air!"

"Yeah, sure," said Blake, rolling his eyes in disbelief. The others ignored Joe.

Blake turned to Leo. "Like I said, if you can't make a basket, get out of here!" he said in an ugly voice.

Frowning, Leo tossed the ball toward the basket. But another boy, Jared, hit his arm, making the ball miss the rim entirely.

*What a mean trick!* Piper fumed.

"Air ball!" yelled Blake. Everyone laughed except Leo and Piper.

Piper caught the ball as it bounced away and tossed it through the hoop. The boys stared.

"How'd you do that?" Blake asked Leo.

"I—I don't know," Leo answered.

"That's what happened with the dog!" Joe said fearfully. "There's a ghost around here!"

"I'm not afraid of any ghost," Jared boasted.

Piper picked up the basketball off the ground, ran back a little way, and tossed it right at Blake, Jared, and Joe. Their eyes opened wide with fear. "Let's get out of here!" yelled Jared. The three dashed off down the sidewalk. Leo smiled.

Piper walked thoughtfully across the street, back to her house. Sabrina had said Joe was playing a mean trick. *Isn't that what I've been doing? Playing mean tricks?* she asked herself.

Piper's face flushed with shame. Then she noticed that the silver shoes were looser. They didn't hurt anymore. "I've got it!" she said out loud. "These shoes are for doing good things, not bad. I understand now!"

Piper ran into her garage, took off the shoes, then raced inside. The birthday party was over. Everyone had left. Wrapping paper littered the floor. Dirty plates and cups cluttered the table.

"Where were you?" her parents asked together. "We were worried!"

"We had a surprise birthday party, but it wasn't much fun without you," said Taylor sadly. "I missed you."

"I'm sorry," said Piper. "I helped Lacy find her puppy, and I helped Leo with his basketball shots." *And I learned a lesson,* she added silently.

After eating cake and opening her presents, Piper took the shoes back to the attic. She put them back in the shoebox and hid it in the jungle of coats. She stood in front of the old mirror, looking at her reflection. Clyde rubbed against her legs and gave a soft meow.

*Maybe I'll show the shoes to Taylor someday,* Piper decided. *It would be good to share their secret.* She closed the door to the attic with a smile. She knew she didn't need the shoes to make her feel special anymore. Inside, she knew she had been all along.